Padre Pio

Saint for Reconciliation

1887–1968

Born in Pietrelcina, Italy

Feast Day: September 23

Patron saint of confessors,
stress relief, and the town of Pietrelcina

Text by Barbara Yoffie
Illustrated by Jeff Albrecht

Dedication

To my family:
my parents Jim and Peg,
my husband Bill,
our son Sam and daughter-in-law Erin,
and our precious grandchildren
Ben, Lucas, and Andrew

To all the children I have had the privilege
of teaching throughout the years.

Imprimatur:
In accordance with CIC 827, permission to publish has been granted on February 5, 2018, by the Most Reverend Mark S. Rivituso, Auxiliary Bishop, Archdiocese of St. Louis. Permission to publish is an indication that nothing contrary to Church teaching is contained in this work. It does not imply any endorsement of the opinions expressed in the publication; nor is any liability assumed by this permission.

Imprimi Potest:
Stephen T. Rehrauer, CSsR, Provincial
Denver Province, The Redemptorists

Published by Liguori Publications, Liguori, Missouri 63057

To order, visit Liguori.org or call 800-325-9521.

p ISBN 978-0-7648-2792-1

Liguori Publications, a nonprofit corporation, is an apostolate of the Redemptorists. To learn more about the Redemptorists, visit Redemptorists.com.

Printed in the United States of America
22 21 20 19 18 / 5 4 3 2 1
First Edition

Dear Parents and Teachers:

Saints and Me! is a series of children's books about saints, with six books apiece in the first four sets. The first set, *Saints of North America,* honors holy men and women who blessed and served the land we call home. The second, *Saints of Christmas,* includes heavenly heroes who inspire us through Advent and Christmas and teach us to love the Infant Jesus. The third, *Saints for Families,* introduces saints who modeled God's love within and for the domestic Church. The fourth, *Saints for Communities,* explores individuals from different times and places who served Jesus through their various roles and professions.

The seven books in the *Saints for Sacraments* series explore eight saints who had great love for the sacraments. John the Baptist baptized Jesus in the Jordan River. Padre Pio helped people make a good confession. Teresa of Ávila was known for her great love of the Eucharist. Philip Neri received the Holy Spirit after praying to God. Louis and Zélie Martin, a married couple, taught their children to serve God and the poor. At an early age, John Vianney wanted to dedicate his life to God as a priest; today he is the patron saint of parish priests. Maximilian Kolbe battled poor health to become a priest and brought God's healing to sick people.

Name the saint who lived in the desert and ate locusts and honey. In this set of books, who was the saint with stigmata? Who began a Carmelite convent dedicated to prayer? Who grew up during the French Revolution? Which saints were the parents of Thérèse of Lisieux? Who volunteered to die in place of a stranger in a prison camp? Find out in the *Saints for Sacraments* set—part of the *Saints and Me!* series—and help children connect to the lives of the saints.

Introduce your children or students to the *Saints and Me!* series as they:

—READ about the lives of the saints and are inspired by their stories.

—PRAY to the saints for their intercession.

—CELEBRATE the saints and relate them to their lives.

Saints for Sacraments

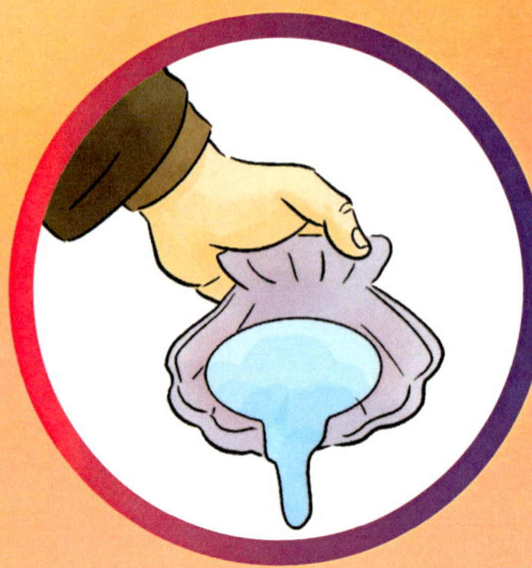

John the Baptist
Baptism

Teresa of Ávila
Eucharist

Philip Neri
Confirmation

Padre Pio
Reconciliation

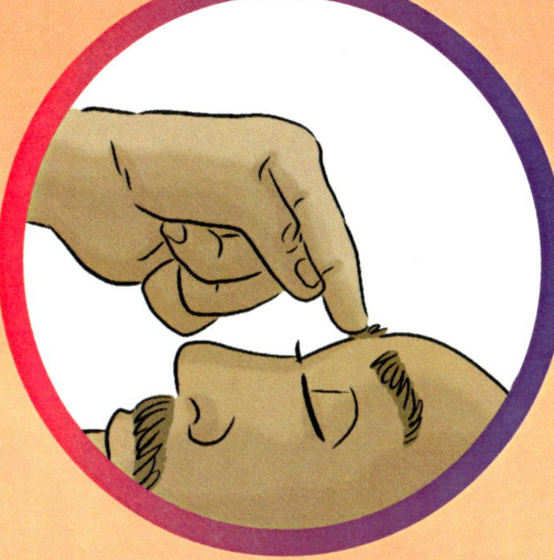

Maximilian Kolbe
Anointing of the Sick

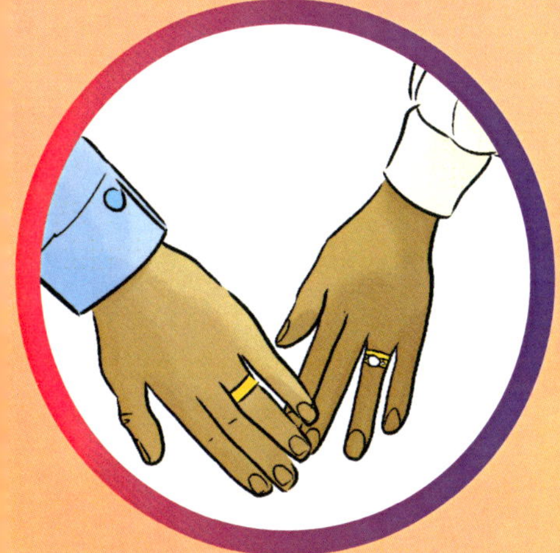

Louis and Zélie Martin
Matrimony

John Vianney
Holy Orders

Padre Pio was an Italian priest and confessor. (*Padre* is "Father" in Italian.) He heard thousands of confessions during his lifetime. Confession, or reconciliation, is a sacrament of forgiveness and peace. Padre Pio filled people's hearts with peace and helped them to love God.

Pio's parents named him Francesco when he was born in 1887. His family went to church every day and prayed the rosary every night. Their Catholic faith was very important to them. Francesco always knew he wanted to be a priest. He loved God and wanted to help people. When he told his parents his goal, they smiled. "You will be a good priest, Francesco, but you will have to study very hard," they said.

So that's what he did! After a few years, he entered the Capuchin friary. His room was small, with only a crucifix, bed, desk, and chair. He wore a brown habit. Francesco was now called Brother Pio. He began his studies for the priesthood. Brother Pio spent many hours praying. He always had a rosary in his hand and a smile on his face. When he was ordained a priest, he whispered to himself, "This is the happiest day of my life!"

Shortly after ordination, Padre Pio became sick and was sent home to rest. When he felt better, he helped the parish priest. He said daily Mass and heard confessions. Padre Pio went to confession often himself. He thought about his sins and prayed for God's forgiveness. The sacrament gave him peace and comfort. He wished everyone could know the great joy it brought him.

A few years later, Padre Pio was sent to the town of San Giovanni Rotondo, where he was a teacher and spiritual director. He told people to pray and look for God in all things. To encourage Catholics to go to Mass daily and confession weekly, he said, “You need to dust a room every week, even when the door is closed.” He urged them to be sorry for their sins so they could make a good confession and be filled with God’s grace.

When Padre Pio said Mass, he prayed very slowly. He thought about how Jesus suffered on the cross. He felt very close to Jesus during Mass. People came from far and near to Padre Pio's Mass because they wanted to feel close to Jesus, too!

One day, while praying after Mass, Padre Pio was surprised to see someone standing in front of him. He was scared. He looked at his hands and feet, and he felt his chest. *"What is happening?"* he wondered. Padre Pio had the wounds of Jesus on the cross, just like St. Francis of Assisi!

The wounds of Jesus, called the stigmata, were a special gift from God. Padre Pio joined in Jesus' suffering and felt his pain. This special gift was very hard to explain. God gave him other gifts as well, such as the gifts of healing people and knowing things about the past and the future.

Padre Pio used some of his special gifts when he heard confessions. Many times he knew what people were going to say. He knew what was in their hearts. When people tried to hide sins, he would tell them all about it. Sin hurts our friendship with God and others. Confession brings those friendships back.

Sometimes people weren't prepared for confession. Sometimes they weren't sorry for their sins. Padre Pio would send them away, saying, "Come back when you are truly sorry!" Most of the time, people were sorry. They confessed their sins. Padre Pio forgave them in Jesus' name. They felt God's love and peace in their hearts. They felt Padre Pio's great care and concern.

His love for people included the poor and the suffering. His big dream was to build a hospital. Lots of people donated money to build the Home for the Relief of Suffering in San Giovanni Rotondo. It opened in 1956. Today it is one of the largest hospitals in Italy, helping thousands of people each year.

Besides helping people, he prayed for them. Every day he offered Mass for others and he prayed several rosaries asking Mary to help them. He spent quiet time alone with God. Padre Pio often said, “Pray, hope, and don’t worry.” If we follow his advice, we will grow closer to God.

Padre Pio was always close to God. Before he died, he renewed his Franciscan vows and made his last confession. He held his rosary in his hand and prayed the words "Jesus, Mary" over and over until his last breath. Now he is in heaven with God, Mary, and all the saints, praying for us.

People around the world loved Padre Pio. He changed the lives of many people. By encouraging prayer and frequent confession, he brought them back to God and the Church. Padre Pio, one of the greatest saints of all time, was canonized by Pope John Paul II in 2002.

Please don't rush and do not hurry,
Pray and hope and do not worry.

Saint Padre Pio,

you helped many people

through your

prayers and advice.

Help me to remember

to pray for others—

especially those who

are sad or hurting. Amen.

GLOSSARY (New Words)

Brother: A male member of a religious order who takes special vows

Capuchin: A member of a religious community founded by St. Francis of Assisi

Canonize: To declare a person to be a saint

Confessor: A priest who hears confessions

Friary: A community where Franciscans live

Grace: The gift of God's life in us

Ordination: To receive the sacrament of holy orders and become a priest

Sacraments: The seven special signs of God's life and love

San Giovanni Rotondo: A town near the southeast coast of Italy

Spiritual director: A person who guides people in their faith

Stigmata: The five wounds of Jesus appearing on the hands, feet, and side of a person